Praise for Where

Full of gem-cut details, Ha... word. A pebble or a pie or a clos... saster. Hazlett can turn the complex simple, as the be... do. She reveals the raindrops held by the cloud. —*Kevin Rabas, Poet Laureate of Kansas (2017-2019), More Than Words*

These are poems on the dark side, for the most part, the lonely side, every line carefully crafted and paid for. They are poems of resilience too. At the heart of this collection is a sequence of "prom dress" poems, in which the poet artfully catches, in the elaborate descriptions of the prom dresses, the lives of these girls at one of their most hopeful moments. I see the making of these poems as the artistic response of the poet to life often broken like a snapped necklace, the beads picked up and meticulously repaired. The repair of the necklace mirrors the repair of the persona's mind. If the beautiful protagonist of Maupassant's "The Necklace" had, instead of working herself to the bone, written sad, beautiful poems about loss, then we might have seen poems like this, in which something vital is saved by the writing of lines shimmering with a thousand beads.— *Brian Daldorph, editor of Coal City Review*

In Where Have You Been?, Sandy Hazlett, by crafting imagery with words and syntax chosen with exquisite care, reveals an ability to open world's one wants, no, needs to explore, that leave the reader stunned at nearly every turn of the page. New layers of meaning and intent appear over and over. There are so many memorable phrases in these poems, such a unique and creative lexicon from which she draws her lyrics.

Poem after poem gives us the experience of new ways of seeing the world, new insights, and new perspectives.
—*Roy Beckemeyer, The Currency of His Light*

Poem by poem, Sandy Hazlett composes an ancient but still-radical argument: there is no difference between loving the shattered world and attending lovingly to its smallest shards — glass beads, old chicken droppings, the body's betrayals, the "persistent basso" of late winter. "It all becomes one thing."
—*Eric McHenry, author of Odd Evening, Poet Laureate of Kansas (2015-2017)*

Sandy Hazlett's Where Have You Been? takes us through real and imagined journeys, from sailing to flights of mind, and to all the different paths we might have taken and where they might have led. These poems engage with other writers, artists, and even dance as they convey loves and losses and the aching silences of homes. Here, at the edge of these days, "shadows fall over the pages," but so does light and hope. Through a varied use of form and persona, Hazlett shows us where she has been, where she's imagined, and what journeys might still lie in wait.
—*Traci Brimhall, Poet Laureate of Kansas (2023-) author of* Come the Slumberless to the Land of Nod

WHERE HAVE YOU BEEN?

WHERE HAVE YOU BEEN?

POEMS

Published in 2024 by Anamcara Press LLC

Author © 2024 Sandy Hazlett
Book design by Maureen Carroll; cover photo by Sandy Hazlett
Georgia, Timeburner, and Minion Pro.
Printed in the United States of America.

Book Description: A collection of poems.
The Prom Dress Room was published by Anamcara Press as a
fundraiser for the Social Service League of Lawrence, Kansas, in
2017

ANAMCARA PRESS LLC
P.O. Box 442072, Lawrence, KS 66044
https://anamcara-press.com/

Ordering Information:
Quantity sales. Special discounts are available on quantity
purchases by corporations, associations, and others. For details,
contact the publisher at the address above.
Orders by U.S. trade bookstores and wholesalers. Please contact
Ingram Distribution.

Hazlett, Sandy, Author
Where Have You Been?

[1. POETRY / Subjects & Themes / Place. 2. POE023010
POETRY / Subjects & Themes / Death, Grief, Loss.

ISBN-13: 978-1-960462-45-9 (Paperback)

ISBN-13: 978-1-960462-46-6 (Hardcover)

Library of Congress Control Number: 2024909322

In memory of my father and mother:
Theodore Lyle Hazlett Jr. (1918-1979)
and Susan Brimmer Inches Hazlett (1926-1981)
who often asked me, with dismay,
"where have you been?"
For Adam and Josh
and For Jake

For you, reader,

I share the last words my father said to me:
"Everything is going to be all right".
He was right, you know,
Everything is going to be all right.

Contents

Appreciations

It takes many people to make a book. I am grateful to:

My "blurbers" who read these poems and wrote such beautiful commentary: Keven Rabas, Brian Daldorph, Roy Beckemeyer, Eric McHenry, and Tracy Brimhall.

Those who went one step further, sat with me over coffee and made suggestions for the manuscript: Ronda Miller, Brian Daldorph, Dennis Etzel, and Iris Craver.

Denise Low Weso for her exceptional and humbling editing. Micki Carroll of Anamcara press for her patience and encouragement from *The Prom Dress Room* to *Where Have You Been?*

The Second Sunday Goes Fourth writing group in which many of these poems were written.

Ilya Kaminsky and Katie Farris for their (unbeknownst to them) mentorship. Ilya taught a class I attended at the Iowa Summer Writing Festival and Katie's book, Standing in the Forest of Being Alive, was not only read many times, but was carried everywhere as a test book for my dust jacket.

Rick Mitchell for his suggestions and help with the photographs.

Tim O'Brien for teaching me letterpress and helping me make the dust jacket.

Mark King for making the fences at my farm. The one outside my kitchen door is on the dust jacket.

ART HISTORY

Art History

Each blue period
whitewashes my past
like the Madonnas
of Firenze Restaura—
one canvas spanning eras,
layers laid bare:
Byzantine-eyed Madonna,
Gothic lip,
Renaissance half smile,
making a Pop Magdalene.

Layers have made of me
a restoration project,
scraped and salvaged
from floods and soiled airs.
One canvas,
one life,
remembered wholly.
Illness is an art.

Breaking

It was there the necklace broke
there on the walk between my front door
and the car that will take me to the hospital.
Just a wave of the hand
the string breaks its clasp.
Beads drop and scatter
each bead a bit of life:
Silver-etched with paired fish or lone florets,
black-and-white Venetian trading beads,
turquoise gone green from oily fingertips,
coral, carnelian, and Peking glass.

They lose themselves in the primrose
beneath the unpruned Hawthorn.
They mingle with coral berries.
I gather as many as I can.
These beads in my hand
will be taken to the jeweler
while I see the dazzling doctors
try to rethread my mind.
But, each time, there is a missing gem.
Three becomes two.
I count
my losses one stone at a time.

Perch Level

After a great shock
hens roost timidly
at perch level:

Two unscathed Reds on top,
the roughed-up Barred Rock
on the lowest rung,

the wing-broken Leghorn
on the platform
of old droppings.

I face my day
at perch level too—
the height of the black dog.

She Was Breaking

She was breaking
computer codes
seeing a swell
of shiny cars
and dark windows.
At Lone Star, one car
"filled with gypsies," she said
disturbed the voices
in her head.
For hours we walked
though she hadn't slept
in weeks since
she fell in love
with an eco-terrorist.
Never mind
this day was soothing.
She left me artisan bread
filled with fruit and nuts.
Her mind
dwelling on delusion,
she got into her Element
and drove back to Kansas City.

Haiku 2

On the Christmas tree
a shiny red ball hangs down
I look very fat.

Toys

My childhood sits on a shelf in a sailing ship.
Sammy has fallen. Wifey sleeps at the mast.
Mousey looks off the port side,
awake to where the wind wills.
A wooden angel steers, facing astern.

I study them as if looking for a message
like coins thrown in I-Ching—
the significance of the sail,
the wind, the water.
        adrift
in the hands of a blind guardian.

This Gentle Madness
for John Clare

To be present
condemns a mind
as
instability seeps
under floorboards,
creeps down
from thatch and mud—
A laborer peasant
with all
the sensitivity of a poet
on scraps of paper
hidden in his pockets
out on those lonely hills.

My Jar of Buttons

Button, button, who's got the button?
    This one is from my red cardigan
    I wore in the fifth grade
    at Fox Chapel Country Day School.

Button, button, who's got the button?
    The plain dark green from my uniform
    at the Ellis School
    with button down shirts, belts, 1 inch wide,
    brown oxfords that tied.

Button, button, who's got the button?
    Here is a pink, satin-covered button
    from my formal dress
    I wore to prom
    with Martin and the theme "Under the Sea".

Button, button, who's got the button?
    This one is from my wedding dress.
    It closed the lace in back.
    Here it is, although the dress is gone—
    and the marriage.

Button, button, who's got the button?
    I am looking for one
    from the blouse my mother wore
    when she ended her life
    but it is not here.
Button, button, who had the button?

SECRETS

Secrets

Secrets sit on my windowsill
like a fresh cherry pie.
Sweet smells of fruit and butter
drift to the trees.
Censers wafting incense
fill the house
sensed by anyone
who happens to be
on one side
or the other.

Ned's Point Lighthouse

A lighthouse at the end of a dark lane
overlooks granite lined with quartz,
beauty and danger, intermittent sight.

We are

down a remembered stairway. Count.
Sea air lifts a wing,
squalls up toward the light.

We are not

Voices. Down here they rise
out of a crack in the foundation,
whisper what everyone needs to know.

We are not hollow

My name goes by voice and word.
All understanding is hung on a hook
by the door, a heavy coat, a scarf.

We are not hollow playthings

Here, nothing is needed but the bare body,
the willingness to let it move
where it needs to go.

We are not hollow playthings of forgotten hands.

The New Bedford Whaling Museum

Boat by boat
over the ambergris
coiled roped spears
held high
searching deep waters where the last bloody fin dove
under waves
far from the bethel
where sailors lie.

Bone on bone
no oil lit rooms,
their lockers left,
wrapped in gauze,
frayed gray remains
of harbor ropes
sticking to the barnacled hull
asking for emergence,
for a following.

The sting of salt on cut hands
throws home the last harpoon
until the body bobs,
bladder defied,
floats against the starboard side.

Axe cut hunks of meat and blubber
melted hot oil for lamps
by which sailor's etch
ghosts of home,
bone on bone.

Solitude

The wind speaks to me at the panes,
knocks from where it came.

Leaves blow on the deck.

Small pebbles are thrown at the window
like a lover wanting to come in.

The crystal clock ticks.

The house aches
with percussive heat.

The sound of silence is at home
gnawing from the inside.

Buddha Dances

What stands between me
    and mystery?
If tears enter there,
    stop seeking.
If laughter enters there,
    come and go.
I stay behind open windows
    looking out onto fields.
While Buddha dances,
I am the one who turns to stone.

The End Of "Reading John Ashbery"

If it weren't for this island of catatonia
I could move my hand over your cheek,
whisper—my heart beating faster—
wet wonder and anticipation.

If it weren't for this catatonia I could love you.
I could write you a poem,
but there is an aura here, a halo
that lies still in silence.

The magic lantern is lit and turns
shadows on the wall.
Through the shadows I can love you well
in spite of this island of catatonia.

If it weren't for this melancholy,
for these wild shifts of desire,
I would call this love poem #6.

Bowsprits

Oh, how I love the girls of yesterday,
their bosomy abundance
adorned in pearls, chinkling chains,
their trinketed lobes and bejeweled fingers,
a ring of them, encircled
by red-glossed, gossipy grins.

How they chit and chat
together like a proud fleet,
these women staring straight at the stem
daring time to unanchor them.

Exposed port and starboard,
spread legs at birth and arms at death,
wiser than the mizzen,
their endurance overwhelms
less travelled youth.

See how their knits fall abast, tunic-like,
over swollen hips,
to hide the carriage of years,
the cargo in the hold,
testimony tucked in a log of thighs
and sighs that surround those they love.

They caress the air with gestures that suck in the sea.
Though their draft is lowered now,
their heads hold high
as they plow the rest of us through.

You will see them when
it is your turn
to step ashore.

Out Of The Wind

for Jake

Since we don't share the weighty things of life
we spend hours lightly touching.

Words lie just beneath the surface of my skin.
Your feathery touch over my body lifts

morning pillow words through darkness, airborne,
like performers in Cirque du Soleil.

You may be the milkweed I gave you—
one breath and you'll be gone

with the grace of a Sandhill Crane passing through
(though we know cranes pair for life).

I hold my breath and lie beside you.
I kiss the sharp, boney wing of your shoulder.

Out of the wind, this is enough luck for now.

Today, without my asking, you hold me tightly.
You leave an extra coat on my porch.
We plan a garden and a trip to the county fair.

TRACKING

Thick

Confusion is thick like low-lying trees.
An owl disturbs the air and flies to pines.

Thickets and tangles of mean stories are retold and
believed.
Fairy tales manage our adult lives. It's hard to break
the spell.

Call the armies of radical acceptance. The outlook is
not good. Knots of wood are useless entreaties to a
god of forgiveness

begging for mercy. I have taken again to supplication.
Words leave easily but the second Bach minuet remains.

Air is thick in the cerebellum. How do I live?
Forcing the issue, the tissue, the tweed of daily chores:

these simple motions protect the fragile heart.
My brain pan has gone empty while there is more
terror in the world.

I read writers from Ukraine, women, writers losing
language. So much in this world. So much no longer
in this world.

Shadows fall over pages, under a full, crisp, moon.
Here is a warm retreat under thick covers of this
man's body.

Tracking

Knock on the door of reason.
Stand there as long as it takes.

Don't make a sudden move.
Be noiseless on morning's ground.

Take cover before bear traps open and the fan's whir
stirs up memories of summer cricket calls

behind wood furniture.
Tune up the siren call. Take to the hills.

Where do all of the flowers go?
Why can't I go home?

You walk on the path to nowhere and wonder why you
are lost.
That is the answer you see. Stable feet on the ground.
Make it yours. Come home.

The other side of the journey makes a parallel story.
Keep tracking in the snow, the black marks of ink across
the page.

You can tell which kind of animal, where it is going, how
fast.
Predator or prey.

One Thing

Brown vines in warm weather
climb the dead arbor under a morning moon.
Icy slush holds weight on the pond,
lacy edges, pitted pockets of water.

A hawk flies low into the woods
pitching perfect angles
in the gray, wet air.
Everything is mud and clay and manure.

Trails from shoe bottoms mark every path.
Compost is upheaved.
I am sinking in the low moon mud
bitterly uncovered by weed and sod.

My eye is on the tambourine spring
as late winter plays its persistent basso.
The gravel is gray. The sky's face.
It all becomes one thing.

Radical Hope In The Sere

The world is sufficiently dry,
dry enough
to wipe your tears
the moment you understand
muses have all gone to shadow.

In the desert of last days,
old Quakers wait
on wooden benches
in meeting houses,
white and green and stone
dry to the bone.

It is dry enough to end the singing,
dancing fields,
canvas flashes of brush and paint,
reason's grip,
straight lines of numbers.

Time's arrow pierces curves,
finding wars in sand,
dry enough to soak up blood,
and send the sirens screaming.

In the halo of this world
keep your eye on the oasis
even though you don't know
if it is real
or if it is an illusion.

Creation

From low-slung muck and ooze
helical angels, the messengers,
arc in spiral ladders
making divergent replicas,
migrating mutations.

Forms that passed through the sea
to the vegetal network
of seed and blossom.

Forms that crawled
and stood on hillsides,
saying "mine."

With an intelligence that is dumb to the land
they bowed to an other knowing:
a dead creator
whose body is the wafer that softens
the tongue.

At The Edge Of The Day

At the edge of the day
mapping Terra Incognita
sailors swoon over finned beasts
before the fall.

At the edge of the day
light lets go her hold
and shakes the hand of evening.
In grace they pass each other by.

At the edge of the night
stars remember their birth
and huddle together in stories
for the ones who look upwards.

At the edge of the night
a barbed-wire curtain cuts coyote,
and owl marks her prey
while we gather our prayers,

supplicants asking to see
the edge of the following day.

EVERYDAY RESURRECTIONS

Sometimes There Are No Words

to describe what happened in the past.
A child forgets in syllables
but remembers in skin
whether the air was hot or cold,
a hug or a turned back.

They say time will tell
but, sometimes, it is silent
or speaks in a different language
whose translation changes stories.

Memories are only from photographs
but the smell of the Earth
returns and the feel of seashells.
The mouth wants to speak of when—

Carnival

After the accident, life was not the same.
One moment, then another.

Sympathy marks its way forward
on a hesitant path

like on a float at Carnival.
Throw bright beads and candy.

Toss something more significant as you go—
and you do go.

This day is colorful and shiny,
tomorrow fasting and penitent.

Masks surround you,
look at you,
at your mask, which looks back.

Pecans

In a blue-moon month once
resplendent grass lies indolent under snow.
It does not know Spring will come.

What hope lies there so silently,
faded like the flowers for the season
and burrowing furs?

He said to me, "It will be OK",
my father dying,
my husband comforting.

In my middle age
I crawl over the ground
gathering hope like the last pecans.

A few months ago this tree was full and green,
its fruits gone now except a few rotten ones
the squirrels have left.

Under the leaves I find a smooth, hard shell.
I crack it open to invaginated folds
of blackish brown and rusty crimson
like the labial lips of an old woman.
I lick the bitter fruit and toss it into the rotting leaves.
It will not take root this Spring.

This body is bleeding from the inside.
Wounds do not heal.
They last and mark the moon.

Fall

It's a leaf-down
leaf-down
leaf-down
raking-down day.

It's a way to outwit
the witless mind,
mind you,
an exercise in fall colors,

the tarp and pull,
drag and heap,
compost to keep away
the sneaker's edge of a shudder
that rustles close to the skull.

Meditation #7

If you bring your mind
to an early winter
you will see
nests in the trees.
You will see
your neighbor's land
is not very different from
your own.

Re: Joyce In The Morning
for Alison Dishinger

Crow cries in the distance.
Another answers from further away.
This breakdown of language
may just be ravages of a syphilitic mind,
a testament of deranged devotion,
an iron-on patch in the plug of an eye—
in the blink of—.
Out on the lawn, a clatter of crows,
pitched whistles of songbirds.
*

We lost power this morning but no time
according to the clock on the stove.
The sea is tracking home her foam,
wave after wave in the impossibly vast
space of time. What a waste.
He has come down from the gun rest,
said the prayers of early morning,
and given them to me to put in safe keeping.
Let me wait another day—
how much more waiting and how many days?—
*

Grasp the bird's tail, left and right,
slow motion on bent knees
to welcome the morning,
to move this body forward
over red vinyl tiles on the kitchen floor,
far from that infamous, old harbor.

ABECEDARIAN

As I sit here waiting
By the window
Closest to the door,

Dying a little in that
Empty space where you had been
Forever in my vision

Giving me sight and solace
Holding my gaze in yours.

I miss you.

Just as you used to be so near to me
Knowing every part of me,
Limb to limb and body to body.

My very own paramour.
Now sword and shield are left
Over by that corner window
Perhaps to be taken up again in a
Questionable dream.

Rare hopes
Sustain me day to day.

Today, in your shadow,
Under the skylight's canopy,

Violet surrounds me
While I still wait as for an

Xmas present. It is
Your presence I desire, you the
Zenith of my heart.

Everyday Resurrections

Last night's blouse,
crumbs in the pocket,
wine stain on the breast,
scoured; it hangs
under the sun,
arms outstretched,
pin to pin.
At the end of the day
I bring it in.
It is bleached and stiff.
I press it to my face
as if
I had brought down a savior
and she were still alive.

OCCASIONAL POEMS

Lunch Buffet

for Cyrus
who doesn't know me

Today was my first day out after surgery.
I went to the library and then to the Indian restaurant
which serves my favorite lunch buffet.
As I was eating my first plate full,
a poet I knew walked in,
like a normal person with his wife and two children.
When I got up for seconds he was there,
just the two of us in front of the curries.

I said his name as a question.
He looked at me with friendly curiosity.
I told him my name followed by…poetry readings…
He smiled and nodded as he spooned raita, "ah, yes"
he said, as if remembering me.
I mentioned how I was pleased to have seen his name
in a mutual friend's novel,
"the future poet". He was honored.
We agreed how much we like this Indian buffet.
He said he comes here when he visits his parents in
Topeka.

I nodded.
I did not tell him that his father was my psychiatrist.
He wouldn't remember me either.
I did say how I always eat too much
and he said, "yes, I do too, one plate too many."

After we agreed on this, I carried my plate back to my
seat, satisfied,
as if he had acknowledged that, as poets,
we were equals.

Finding Out Cancer

For Nancy and Tom

This house will stand
against worm and wind.
Light will shine
on every room
filled with the stuff
of love and a life
together. This house will stand
against the body's violent weather.
Hand in hand
This house will stand
and this house will stand
tomorrow.

Reconciliation
Eulogy for Rex Powell (8/13/42-3/14/2019, Pi Day)

He would have wanted a poem
to be free of the written word
to sing
to listen to silences
to reach the stars

He made his home at Burton's Hollow
not too far from his child's Lone Star
or where you and I are.

He built his nest among the trees
within the woods and of the woods—
bird song, possum shuffle, owl call, rain.

He loved passionately with purr and claw
Mother Earth and all of hers
to the sky, the Milky Way, the universe.

He was always a teacher
    "For the children! For the children!"
Loud beyond words the stories I heard
from his body, of his body.
His penciled eyebrows held me there,
signing hands and genuflection
until his whole body laughed or cried
or screamed the life of this dying earth.

He took me out to show me the night sky
I lay in the back of his pickup truck
watching meteor showers.
He taught me
to slightly unfocus my eyes
to see the brilliant falling.

He took me out to dig clay for fossils,
to listen to the morning sandhill cranes,
to walk the native prairie.
Just down from the old cemetery's Iris and Peony
he took me to see one prairie fringed orchid
he tried to save from the plow.

He brought us all together
for parties under the full moon
by the fire
potluck
margaritas and stories.

Yes, he had his bully nature.
He polished his ego
to dim what he secreted as his lesser lights.
He bragged about the size of his
telescope.
He would rage and rant
throw tantrums at the world's wasting.

Then he would invite us in:
"Here,
taste this tea.
Listen to the birds at the feeder
See the silence of the woods.
Here,
hold this rock, this meteorite, this fossil, this shell—
and I will tell you its story."

Finally, I see his Wall of Reconciliation,
his monument to the best of humankind,
harmony of the body, the mind, the spirit
all one.
This is his testament:

"Find your hollow.
Make your home.
Be that place
from rock to plant to creature to star.
Keep safe where you are
and love,
love it all with all you are."

Listen to what he was telling you,
"Oh sweetie, you can do it."
He is still telling you.
Listen.

FLASH POEMS

A Moth In The Salt

A mother in the salt
in the wound makes the hurt
harness memories at the table.
At the table of my heart
she comes again, shaken
by her unseasonable life
which she took for herself
into her soul's cellar
in the salt, in the common sand
of the sea.
Now she makes me
wish for a grain of love —
my arms reach out in a crawl,
push against waves
that push back
far from shore,
from even the possibility
of mother in the salt of the earth.

Perhaps Your Wolf Has Done All She Can For You & Has Moved On

With my grandmother still in her belly
my wolf has moved on.
The axe man has gone
and left me with my hood,
red mood, and missing her.
I set traps
springs in trees
leg hobbles.
My wolf, my wolf
missing in the wood.
"Cunning" is a word my grandmother said
for "dear" or "darling" or "quaint,"
not sly like the wolf
who consumed her
but does not know
she will turn herself inside out
and come back to me
while the wolf has moved on,
skin to sky,
howling for what was left undone.

Crackerjack Sweetheart

Martin was my crackerjack sweetheart
though his favorites were Sweet-Tarts.
He had a mind quicker than carnival ducks
all lined up in a row passing at speeds
outsmarting all the shooters
Martin would let the bullets fly,
crack a sugary word, give a quick hug
and send fireworks from my awakening
female lips to the top of my head
like popping corn covered in caramel ooze.
We would schmooze on the roller coaster
getting stuck on the nuts
which proved a good lesson for my future
better than I could hear from the fortune teller
dressed in spangly gauze, looking for money.
But Honey, the future was still waiting then
and Martin, my crackerjack sweetheart,
was full of surprises.

If I Were Male I Would

If I were mail I would send you a letter
since you put me in a box
and stamped me with your approval.
I would be floral prints smelling of roses.

I would envelop myself
in an enclosed secret space
waiting to be licked,
tongue in cheek.

The postman rings more than twice,
gives me parcels and telegrams
before dogs chase him from the screen door.
You know, he told me he would take me too.

The mail comes every day.
I wait for you, for your afternoon post.
Letters, let me become
the woman I wanted to be.

Now it is all email and text and tweet,
not as sweet as paper and pen.
On and off again, we tease with words,
call and response.

If I were male I would be you
and you would receive me in the dull day,
open me,
take up your pen.

Hand-Me-Downs/Sky And Air Earth And Water

Hand-me-down sky
blue and wanting
clear into light
present at dawn
into black night:
Let me lift you up, sky.

Hand-me-down air
in-breath peace
out-breath joy
moving, invisible
connecting all, hand to tree:
Let me keep you clear, air.

Hand-me-down earth
humus under foot
rich furrow of leaf and mold
keeper of bodies
bone and skin and ash:
Let me be your guardian, earth.

Hand-me-down water
cooling presence
fluid, formless
take the shape given
the wave of sea:
Let me keep you pure, water.

Hand-me-down sky. Hand-me-down air and earth. Hand-me-down water. Ours to keep safe, let go, hand down.

Scraps Of Your Life

The scraps of my life
frizzle in hot oil
like hush puppies
for hungry children,
anointed orts
thrown under the table,
the refuse.

I refuse to make do
but I do
as I miss the bright dinner party.
Through the kitchen window
I see Betty sneak hors d'oeuvres
from black-laced trays.

Alone, I watch the paper lantern lights
hanging from trees
over dancing couples
who hold each other tightly
when there is plenty of food,
the drinks keep coming,
and none of them wants for anything.

I Looked At Your Face And Saw

wood for the stove
warm promise
pronghorn-eyed

how you run
cougar's leap
how you climb
roped into the neck
of the oak

the sun circus
high falling dance
snapped up before
ground is hit

you are my net
in this aerial world
your face maps
my celestial twin

your embrace
an indigenous warrior

I feel feather on fur
curtained by fire
by smoke
face to face.

For Jake

THE PROM DRESS ROOM

3D Red

I am venous, anoxic,
iridescent blue/red running under skin.
Deep in shadow and shimmer,
I skim the Andes at sunset,
the rib of a fallen prey.
I am flamenco sumac, autumn viburnum,
shifting fault lines in the earth's core,
glint of sun off a Maori's oar,
red velvet cake under crystal dome,
a perfect glass of port.
Along my back runs an undulant sash,
quiver slant tied to the center fold,
a yawl's rudder trail. Cilia, flagella,
evolution of an armored tail,
princess and dragon rustling as one
down the hewn stone stair.
I am Maillol's Méditerranée,
thick molded thighs,
midnight hair waving on white skin,
mottled as the dress.
We are cut from the same bolt.
I hiss at my mother and baffle my father.
I will study erythrocytes under glass,
perfect dissections, pinned veins on wax.
I will go to medical school, become a surgeon,
master the boney hardness of life.
I marry three men, two Harrys and a Martin.
I leave each one.
My two girls grow to despise me.

I was not made for this man's world.
I set my glare for the one who could be my match.
There are no mirrors here, no stone
but you can almost hear
the hiss of snakes upon my brow.

Crystal Leaf

I hold the center close to my body,
skin soft and thin blurs the edge of cloth,
yellow like tallow, all potential flame.
I am surrounded by crystal leaves,
a Norwegian wood in early winter,
floating over secret folds,
a hint of falling,
falling green leaves.
My dancing ivory ground is the full moon
when no one is watching,
milkweed seed, soft snow.
Hush, hush, the sound of my skirt
against bare legs,
above lightly treading toes.
I am the oldest. I have a younger brother and two
younger sisters.
My mother is bruised and quiet. She drinks sherry
most days
sleeps on the sofa or in her room with the door closed.
I have my own room. I am not allowed to lock my
door.
My father is big and bristly. At night he comes to me,
pushes against me,
covers my mouth and insists in whiskery whispers,
"this is our special secret".
Crying stays inside me, close to me, slippery like tallow, wet and warm,
wrapped in rage until released to run over the forest
floor.

I have not spoken to them in years.
I often wonder about my sisters.
I am a teacher of children in the first grade.
I hold them close, show them how to be safe,
how to see beauty if you know where to look,
how to shimmer without anyone
saying no, saying stop, saying don't.
I never marry.
I live alone.
I live for my first grade children,
for their shine.

Diamond Straps

I mimic Madame X, sleek black with diamond studded straps.
I model the memory of the outrageous slip, off the
shoulder,
the shock of it, Sargent's shame.
I wear my diamonds as they were repainted, high and
wide as my dreams.
I step elegantly into the future,
simple, stately, all line, no commotion,
poise, whispers, silence.
I hide in blackness turned in, no outward ceremony.
It is a matter of state. I will make my mark upon the
world.
I give my valedictory address
overcome with the subtle hint that this,
this now, is the best it would ever be.
Within the year I drop out of college,
sit for days on the sofa
solemn and suicidal.
There is no recovery. I am sent away.
I survive, barely, with the mark of mental illness,
a bit of hope, some surrender, more bitterness.
It never does get any better than that.
I become the fallen diamond strap.

Homemade Sparkling Peach

I have gone gaudy at Hobby Lobby.
I have something to prove
and I mean to show them.
All sanguine and sequins,
I rush against running out,
running out of money, running out of time.
I hear my mother's fears.
How much can I spend and still look ravishing,
(because I will look ravishing)
in my dress for the prom?
I am self made and secure
a 4H trained seamstress to boot.
I go for the vocal bolt,
fabric that confesses, calls,
and happens to be on sale.
A copy of a pattern
to tweak to my size, trim an edge,
I am on it.
My name is Sparkle, I go for the gold
bric-a-brac around my neck.
I keep myself above it, make it short, lots of leg.
I walk into a room like the sunrise.
I will become an entrepreneur
import fabric and handcrafts from the silk road.
I marry a Presbyterian minister. I know it seems odd
but he indulges me.
We get by with a moderately hemmed life.
I make our lives into the future.
For my daughter, I sew her dress for the prom.

Blue Velvet Saks

I am the rich girl, deep in blue velvet Saks and satin,
the Mediterranean's evening sea,
cobalt and lapis lazuli.
I am the silent sapphire of Crater Lake,
the edge of night on the tall grass prairie.
I am the plume of the Aurora, the infinite cerulean
sky.
Within the body of this blue,
I am more manly than you would know
by my graceful step.
I am Tarzan on the playground.
I man the oars and come to the rescue.
Into this depth of blue
I become homeless
to earth and sky.
I live fluid,
just above the meniscus,
just shy of surface tension.
I am both mast and siren.
Up before light, I swim. I swim miles every day,
away from gravity, levitation to the bones.
One, two, breathe. One, two, breathe.
My water waltz, my liquid meditation.
I will win a scholarship with my stroke.
I am Olympic material they say
but my times fall short.
It passes me by.
I arise ordinary, landed.

When my girls are six and nine,
I suffer an aneurism and drown
while on vacation in Vancouver.

Disco Ariadne

I am glamorous,
revolving light,
reflecting outward,
along my sleek and slender form.
I carry silken thread
on the diamond studded
center of my back,
the thread that leads
out of the maze into the light.
I will save you from confusion,
from the darkness.
I celebrate my radiant participation
in the bacchanalian ball of the evening.
Before I step into the next world
of my adulthood let me shine now
so I may remember.
I will go to college. I will study astrophysics,
the web of the glittering universe.
I will meet a man who is an oceanographer.
We will marry and move to Woods Hole.
I shift my interest to the sea, to our coral reefs,
and I dive into the bioluminescent night.
One by one I watch them bleach and die,
mourn their extinguished light.
I can't save them
though they are made
from the same light as I.

Blush

I was the girlie girl,
bubble gum in silver foil,
My Little Pony,
Barbie doll,
pink haired troll.
My dress is heavy to wear.
Over a fine pink satin slip
lies its rosy sheath,
sewn with thousands of beads,
light catching cylinders,
heavy enough to keep me grounded,
to keep me from leaping up,
leaping away.
The cowl draped down my back
becomes a pretty pack
when I finesse my leaving.
I will study painting.
I will make pastel swashes of dancers.
Over and over again I paint
ribbons and satin,
pointed toes,
the urgent power
of their delicate twirl.
I visit Degas at the Louvre,
the foot of Constantine in Rome,
Michelangelo's David.
I confess the most astonishing detail
of Annie Liebovitz in her studio
is the bare foot of Baryshnikov.

I have inherited the gene for Huntingdon's.
My life becomes heavy to wear.
I put my brushes down,
hold my older sister's hand,
and dance the rigid staccato of my limbs.

Orchidaceae

This is not my testament.
I dropped the ball and sent out aerial roots
into the canopy of the Plant Queendom.
Perennial epiphyte, I am in the arms of the mother,
Pachamama.
Jaguar and puma pad below me snarling upward their
curl of sound.
I am blue green of the abundant river,
luminous, fecund, lethal.
This is my ovation.
On the shore of womanhood I search for our begin-
ning,
when matriarchs joined hands in the circle of fathers,
when the blood that flowed from them,
the babies they bore,
the food they gathered and cooked at the fire,
their jungle of words that tied the band together,
all were lifted up in praise and placed in right com-
munion.
I will scatter my studies between anthropology, ar-
chaeology, and ecology
until I hear the question, "should trees have standing?"
I will go to law school for environmental law.
I litigate for the world's women and children,
for the voiceless,
for the flora and fauna of the Amazonian Basin.
I screech and howl to protect the unprotected.
After all, it's a jungle out there.

Solitaire

I am the winter prairie,
broom sedge, little bluestem,
coyote fur, a herding, lone, red heeler.
I am thin skinned, indecisive,
uncomfortable in crowds.
I melt into my dress.
I mimic flesh so I can blend in.
I keep it short so I can walk away.
Clubs, pearls, and lace at my waist,
two lines of thought, subtle decorum.
I am a pleated column.
I will go to nursing school,
join Doctors Without Borders,
travel to the Caucasians.
I will meet a handsome intern
who marries me when I become pregnant.
I raise his two sons. He never loves me.
We retire to Coral Gables, Florida.
The doctor dies peacefully in his reading chair.
I sneak cigarettes in the bathroom
and eat scrambled eggs with ketchup
because there is no one to tell me not to.
I have chronic catarrh and spit into the coconut tree.
In my pearl slippers on terra-cotta tile
I shuffle cards in a metal box
and play solitaire in the sunroom.

Notes and Acknowledgements

All poems written before 2015 were written under my name at the time, S. Hazlett Mitchell or Susan Hazlett Mitchell. Poems after 2015 were written under my current name, Sandy Hazlett.

"Art History" first appeared in *Coal City Review,* Issue #20, January 2005. Firenze Restaura was a project of restoration of Florentine artwork that had been devastated by flooding. I was in Florence in 1972 and saw posters for this project all over the city. The poster was a palimpsest of Madonnas from periods of Florentine art history.

"Breaking" first appeared in *I-70 Review,* Issue#2, 2004.

"Haiku #2" first appeared in The *Lawrence Journal World,* 12/26/2006.

"Toys" first appeared in *365 Days: A Poetry Anthology* by The 365 Day Poets (2016, 365 Days Poetry, Roy Beckemeyer, James Benger, Dan Pohl, Diane Wahto, Editors).

"Secrets" first appeared in 365 Days:A Poetry Anthology by The 365 Day Poets (2016, 365 Days Poetry, Roy Beckemeyer, James Benger, Dan Pohl, Diane Wahto, Editors).

"The End of "Reading John Ashbery"" was a journal entry written while I was sitting outside a cafe in Lawrence,Kansas and reading John Ashbery's *Self Portrait in a Convex Mirror.* The writing suddenly turned itself into this poem.

"Bowsprits" first appeared in *Coal City Review,* Issue #24, 2007.

"Carnival" first appeared in *365 Days:A Poetry Anthology* by The 365 Day Poets (2016, 365 Days Poetry, Roy Beckemeyer, James Benger, Dan Pohl, Diane Wahto, Editors). It is dedicated to Doug Hitt.

"Meditation #7" first appeared in *I-70 Review,* Issue #1, Volume 3.

"Joyce in the Morning"- My friend, Alison Dishinger, and I share a love for James Joyce's *Ulysses.* Alison also has a passion for typewriters.

"Everyday Resurrections" first appeared in *Quattrocento: An Independent Journal of the Arts* Made in Wales, Issue #2, summer/autumn 2005.

"Lunch Buffet": The poet referred to is Cyrus Console and the reference to his friend is Ben Lerner and his book, *The Topeka School.* I wrote "mutual friend"but, in truth, Ben Lerner doesn't know me either. I do know him and several people in *The Topeka School.*

"Reconciliation": I read this Eulogy for my dear friend, Rex Powell, at his memorial service on March 24, 2019. A recording of the reading is on YouTube under, "Not a Poem, for Rex".

All of the poems in the section, Flash Poems, first appeared in the anthology, *Flash Poems:Poetry and Prompts,* by the Second Sunday Goes Fourth Writing Group, Lawrence, Kansas (2018, Anamcara Press).

Flash poems are poems written to a prompt in about 10 minutes and then shared with the writing group.

The Prom Dress Room first appeared in Coal City Review, Issue #36, 2015. It was published by Anamcara Press, August 2015.

"Solitaire" also appeared in The Shining Years, Poems About Aging (2021,Blue Wild Indigo Productions, Gary J. Lechliter, Editor).

The Prom Dress Room was a fundraiser for the Social Service League of Lawrence, Kansas where I was a volunteer. As I sorted through prom dresses, donated to the League, they began to tell their stories: who wore this dress, what was her life like, and what became of her? The stories inspired these poems.

"Blush" is dedicated to my dear friend, Gwen Wiens, and in memory of her sisters,

Cindy Wiens and Jan Wiens, who both died of complications due to Huntington's Disease.

"Blue Velvet Saks" is in memory of my grade school best friend, Debbie Williams

Photographs

The photograph on the title page is the house in Pittsburgh, Pennsylvania where I grew up. The children are myself and my older sister, Nancy. It was taken by either my father or my mother.

The photograph on the "For the Reader" page is my older sister and myself, taken around 1961 by Stefan Lorant, author of *Pittsburgh, The Story of an American City* (Authors Edition, Inc. Lenox, Massachusetts. 1964.)

Author photo taken by Jake Vail in Galveston Texas. I took the end page photograph which is of my current home, in the Fall, in Lawrence, Kansas.

About The Author

Sandy Hazlett is originally from Pittsburgh, Pennsylvania where she was surrounded by poets and poetry. When she was in Middle School, her father, Theodore Lyle Hazlett Jr., and Dr. Samuel Hazo started the International Poetry Forum. She has been writing since childhood but she began writing with greater intent and study in 1992 when she moved to Lawrence, Kansas. *Where Have You Been?* is a selection of poems from that time.

Hazlett's poetry has been published in Coal City Review, I-70 Review, and Quattrocento. Her poems have been included in the anthologies, *The Shining Years: Poems* About Aging, *Flash Poems: Poetry and Prompts* by the Second Sunday Goes Forth Writing Group, and *365 Days: A Poetry Anthology* by The 365 Days Poets.

The Prom Dress Room was featured in Coal City Review, Issue #36 , 2015. It was published as a chapbook by Anamcara Press, August, 2015. Poems from this collection were nominated for the Pushcart Prize. Sandy lives on her farm in Lawrence, Kansas.

OTHER BOOKS TO ENJOY
FROM ANAMCARA PRESS

Available wherever books are sold or at:
https://anamcara-press.com/

Thank you for being a reader! Anamcara Press publishes select works and brings writers & artists together in collaborations in order to serve community and the planet. *Your comments are always welcome!*

Milton Keynes UK
Ingram Content Group UK Ltd.
UKHW052238280524
443210UK00008B/101